Physty

To Ms. ~~██████~~
and her students
from

Russell Bellows

(and Physty)

10/14/95

Physty

The True Story of
A Young Whale's Rescue

Written and Illustrated
by Richard Ellis

COURAGE BOOKS

an imprint of
Running Press
Philadelphia, Pennsylvania

Canadian representatives: General Publishing Co., Ltd.,
30 Lesmill Road, Don Mills, Ontario M3B 2T6.

International representatives: Worldwide Media Services, Inc.,
30 Montgomery Street, Jersey City, New Jersey 07302.

9 8 7 6 5 4 3 2 1
Digit on the right indicates the number of this printing.

Library of Congress Cataloging-in-Publication Number 92–54937

ISBN 1–56138–271–X

Edited by Gregory C. Aaron
Cover design by Toby Schmidt
Cover and interior illustrations by Richard Ellis
Author photo by Stephanie W. Guest
Interior design by Stephanie Longo
Back cover photos by Richard Ellis and David Doubilet.
Typography: ITC Garamond Light by Richard Conklin
Printed in Hong Kong.

Published by Courage Books, an imprint of
Running Press Book Publishers
125 South Twenty-second Street
Philadelphia, Pennsylvania 19103

PREFACE

This is mostly a true story. Physty was (and probably still is) a real whale. He really beached himself on Fire Island in April 1981. I made up the parts about the shark and the squid, because nobody has ever seen a shark attack a living whale, and nobody has ever seen a sperm whale hunting. I know that all the parts about people trying to help him are true, because I was one of those people. I got into the water with him, swam up to him, and put my hand on his nose.

When I first saw Physty, I thought he was going to die. He was very ill, so we tried to feed him and give him medicine.

After eight days of rest, we let Physty go. If nothing else has happened to him, he's probably still swimming and diving out there in the deep Atlantic Ocean.

—Richard Ellis
New York City
June 1992

from her nipples? Physty's mother had powerful muscles next to her nipples that forced the rich, thick milk into the corner of his mouth. Physty would not be able to catch his own food for more than two years, so his mother would nurse him for that time.

Whales breathe air, just like all mammals. When whales are underwater, they hold their breath. When Physty wanted to breathe, he stuck his nose above the water. At the end of his nose, on the left side, he had one nostril that was shaped like a skinny letter "S." Sperm whales have only one nostril, but other kinds of whales have paired nostrils—just like yours. When a whale exhales, it blows a burst of air from its lungs out through its nose. This burst of air is called the whale's spout.

Physty's head was almost one-third of his body. Most of his head was actually his nose. Sperm whales have the biggest noses in the history of the world, and the biggest brains, too. Right below his nose, exactly where you would expect, was his mouth. He had a long, narrow lower jaw and no teeth at all. His mother, on the other hand, had two rows of large peg-like ivory teeth in her lower jaw. Physty's teeth would grow in when he was older.

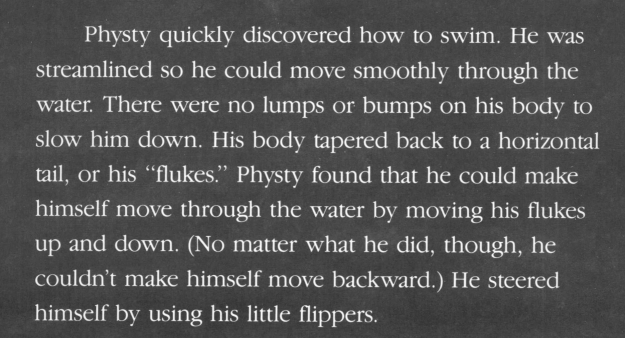

Physty quickly discovered how to swim. He was
streamlined so he could move smoothly through the
water. There were no lumps or bumps on his body to
slow him down. His body tapered back to a horizontal
tail, or his "flukes." Physty found that he could make
himself move through the water by moving his flukes
up and down. (No matter what he did, though, he
couldn't make himself move backward.) He steered
himself by using his little flippers.

Little Physty stayed close to his mother, since she
was his source of food and protection. But one day,

when he was feeling frisky and adventurous, he decided to go off on his own. He swam away from his mother. She called after him, but he was feeling stubborn and independent, and he ignored her.

Physty's mother made clicking sounds to call Physty back to her side. Sound travels well through water, even better than it does in air. Her call sounded like this:

Click . . . . click . . . . click . . . click . . . click . . . clickclick.click.click.click.clickclickclickclickclick.

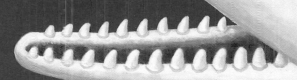

Physty heard her calls, but he kept on swimming, his little tail pumping up and down. His mother could have chased him, of course, but she wanted him to learn that he was supposed to come when he was called.

Unfortunately, another creature also heard the clicks. This animal was *very* curious about these funny noises. It swished its tail from side to side through the water.

It was 20 feet long—longer than Physty. It had a pointed nose, black eyes, and a triangular fin on its back. Its tail was shaped like a quarter-moon, and it had a gaping mouth full of razor-sharp teeth. It was the most fearsome predator in the ocean, a great white shark—and it was hungry.

The shark rose from the depths, using all its senses to home in on the little whale. The shark could see Physty swimming at the surface, and it could hear—and *feel*—the frantic clicks sent out by the mother whale.

Click . . . . click . . . . click . . .
click . . . click . . .
click.click.click.ciick.clickclick
clickclickclickclick.

The shark was swimming
straight toward Physty. But at the same
time that his mother was sending out clicks to
call him back, she was sending out another signal.
These sounds bounced back to her and told her where
Physty was. At first she sensed only Physty, but suddenly

the signals became confused. There was another creature nearby, and it was charging right for her baby!

She whirled into action. With powerful strokes of her flukes, she drove toward Physty and the shark. She was ready to defend her baby with her life.

The shark approached Physty, rolled its eyes back, and opened its jaws, with their rows of sharp teeth.

POW! Physty's mother slammed into the shark with the end of her nose. The shark never knew what hit it. It spun away from the whales, injured, and headed for the safety of the deep.

Physty had had a bad scare. For a long while afterward he stayed very close to his mother. The shark helped him learn to watch for dangers in the ocean.

When Physty was born, his mother was with a
group of other females, some of whom were also giving
birth at that time. There were no males in this family

group, or "pod," since all of them had gone north to hunt for large squid in deeper, colder waters. They would be gone for another eight months. The females (they're called "cows"), and their children (the "calves") stuck together for companionship and safety.

When they were not feeding, the whales rested at the surface. Every time one of them breathed out, a burst of air and water sprayed from her nose. The whales floated peacefully, spouting fountains of mist into the air.

Young whales love to dive and splash, just like you do. Think of how much fun it is to jump into the water. Wouldn't it be great to be able to jump *out* as well? Even adult whales sometimes jump out of the water— it's called "breaching." As with so many things about sperm whales, we don't know why they do it.

The water around the whales was filled with bangs, pings, creaks and squeals. The whales were very noisy. It's possible that their sounds are part of a complex language. If the whales talk to each other, what could they be saying?

When the whales got hungry, they went hunting. Sperm whales eat mostly squid, which live in the cold, dark waters of the deepest oceans. Sometimes the squid live far below the surface, so sperm whales have to dive very deeply. In fact, sperm whales are the champion divers of all mammals. They can hold their breath for an *hour and a half* and dive to two miles below the surface!

Here's one of the things about sperm whales that no one really understands. Two miles down, the water is pitch-black, and it must be painfully cold. So how can whales find the squid they want to eat? Although the whales obviously catch the squid that they eat, we don't have any idea how they do it.

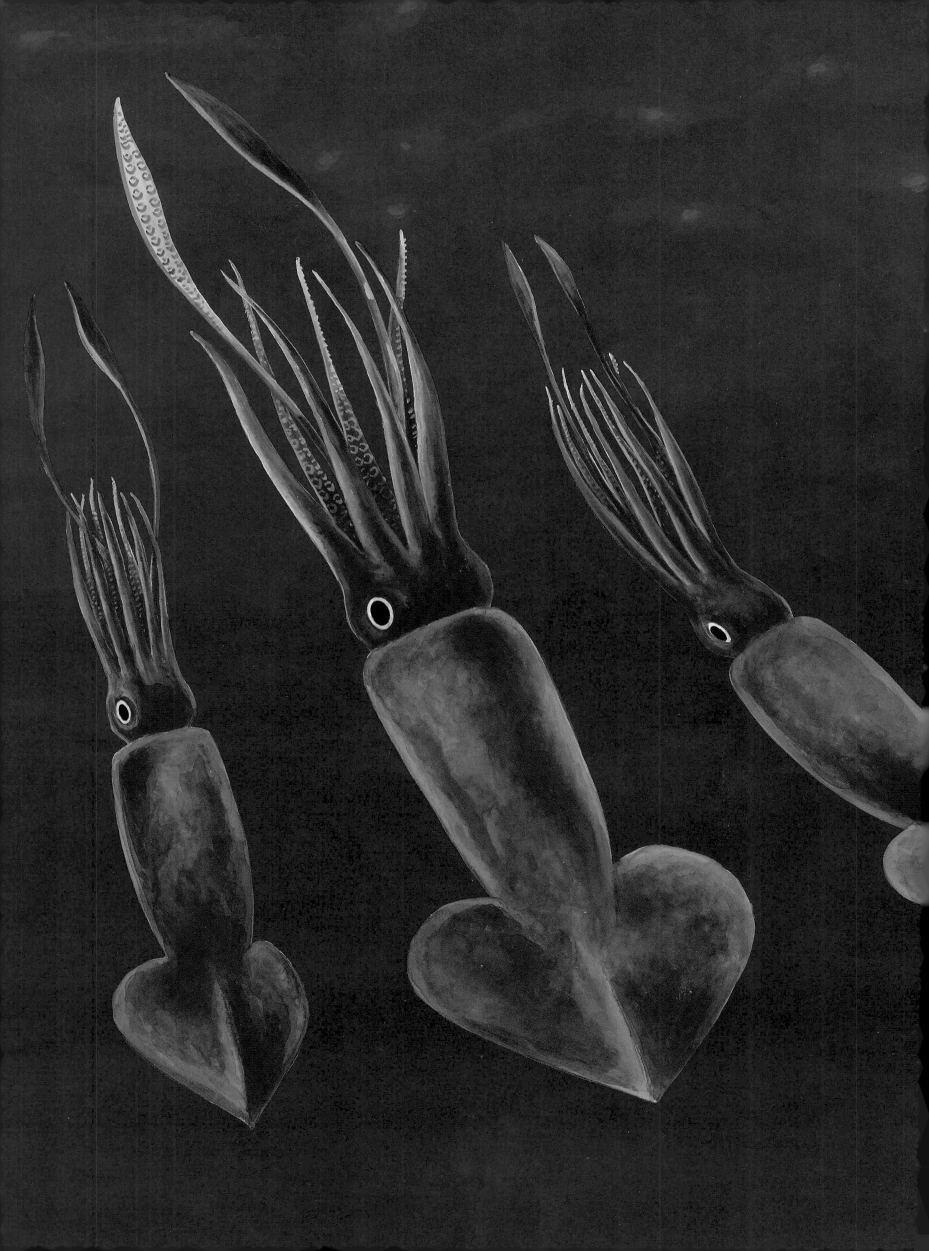

Most squid are two to three feet long, and in order to make a proper meal, the whale has to eat an awful lot of them. It would seem (to us) to be very difficult to catch a lot of fast-swimming squid in dark, cold water—especially when you can't see them, and you have to hold your breath all the time you are trying to catch them.

Imagine you are at a party, and there are dishes of candy on the tables. You would like to have some of the candy, but first your friends blindfold you, and then they hide the candy. To make it even harder, you can only find the candy while you're holding your breath. That's sort of the way a sperm whale has to find its food.

Feeling hungry, Physty's mother prepared to dive. Physty wanted to go with her. They each took a deep breath, then raised their tail flukes into the air and dove straight down. The water was greenish-blue at the surface, but as they swam deeper the water got darker and darker until it was as black as ink. They couldn't see very well, but they could *hear* everything that was going on around them.

For mother and son, hearing was much more important than seeing. No animal can see very well underwater, so whales and dolphins depend almost entirely on their hearing to find food.

Physty's mother made a series of "pings." Her sounds were strong and clear. She was scanning the water around her, waiting for an echo to bounce back. First she heard a sound that signaled there was a gigantic blue whale passing by. Blue whales are the largest animals that have ever lived. This whale was almost *twice* as long as Physty's mother. Different species of whales probably don't have anything to do with each other. So the sperm whales kept on swimming—down, down, down.

There! Physty's mother was getting an echo that told her that there was a large school of squid off to her right.

She turned in the dark so she was facing the source of the sound. Then she began to swim toward it. She kept sending out the "pings" and listening for the echoes. It was dark and cold, and Physty stayed close to his mother.

When she decided she was close enough, she sent out another sound, right at the school of squid. It was a loud *BONG!* It was so powerful that it knocked the squid unconscious. She rushed toward them (she was still holding her breath, remember), and gobbled up as many as she could. Since she couldn't see them, she had to locate them by her "pinging." She was almost out of breath, and even though she knew there were still lots of squid floating around, she headed for the surface. As Physty looked up, he saw the sunlight sparkling on the surface of the water.

Physty's mother swallowed the squid whole (and alive). She did not chew them because sperm whales have teeth only in their lower jaws and none in the upper. If she didn't chew her food and she didn't catch it with her teeth, why did she have teeth, anyway? No one knows. Like so many things about sperm whales, their teeth are a mystery.

When Physty was about five years old, he was still part of his pod, which lived and hunted in the North Atlantic Ocean. Sometimes the pod headed north, as far as Newfoundland, and sometimes it even wandered far across the ocean to the Azores, a group of islands about 900 miles west of Portugal.

Physty had grown to a length of 25 feet. He weighed about five tons (10,000 pounds). He fed on squid by bonging them with his sonic blasts and grabbing them in his mouth before they sank too deep.

That spring, the pod was feeding in the waters off New England. The squid were moving into shallower and shallower water. Physty's mother was still part of the pod, but she and her son did not often swim together. Within the larger group there were other youngsters, some older and some younger than Physty. He tended to hang around with whales of his own age.

One day in April, Physty began to have difficulty breathing properly. He felt sick.

You don't have to worry about where you are when you take a breath. But a whale spends most of its life underwater. If a whale gets into trouble, it has to make sure that whatever else happens, it can get air. (If a whale can't get air to breathe, it can drown, just like any other mammal.) Sick whales sometimes take themselves into shallow water so they can rest on the bottom. This way, they can keep their noses out of the water with little effort.

Because Physty was feeling very sick, he swam to the shore. He found a gently sloping beach and tried to rest. If Physty had been interested in looking up (something whales usually don't do), he would have seen a Ferris wheel, a roller coaster, and other rides. He was at Coney Island.

Coney Island is an amusement park in New York City, and New York City is not a normal place to find whales! Physty was driven into shallower and shallower water by the tide and the surf, until he was almost on the beach. Somebody saw him and called the Coast Guard. The Coast Guard didn't have any idea of what to do with a sick, 25-foot sperm whale, so they towed Physty offshore, hoping he would simply swim back out to sea, where they thought he belonged.

But Physty was too sick to remain in deep water.
That night, he swam along the shore of Long Island
until he found another gentle beach. Forty miles later,
he was on the beach again, at a place called Fire Island.

People had seen Physty on television when he came ashore at Coney Island. When he got to Fire Island, more people came to see him. They knew that Physty couldn't remain on the beach, so they put a rope around his tail and towed him across the bay to a protected boat harbor. The water was so shallow that as he lay on his right side, he kept his blowhole out of the water. He could rest and breathe without moving.

It was the strangest place he had ever been. Physty was used to living in water that was sometimes five miles deep. Now he was in water that was only eight feet deep. He bounced his clicks and pings off the wooden walls of the boat harbor.

But the strangest thing about it were the odd creatures he saw all around him. Each of them had two long skinny arms instead of proper flippers, and no tail at all! And each creature had some sort of a *neck*. Most of the animals that Physty had seen had their heads attached directly to their bodies. It was also surprising that the creatures were able to live out of the water—

Physty could see them standing on the land. When they came into the water, they gurgled and bubbled like no animal Physty had ever seen.

At first the strange little creatures just looked at him. Then some of them came into the water and began to touch him.

One of the creatures was bright red, like a deep-water squid. The red one came up to Physty in the water and placed its hand on the end of his nose. What a strange feeling! The only time Physty had ever felt anything like that before was when a little octopus had crawled over his nose. The little whale sent out some powerful pops, trying to get this object off his nose.

BANG! BANG! The hand came off quickly, and the red creature swam away. Physty could hear some noises, but of course he couldn't understand them.

The man in the red suit said: "He knocked my hand right off his nose!"

A man in a black suit said: "Were the sounds coming from one part of the nose?"

"They seemed to be coming from about halfway down in the middle, you know, where it gets all flattened out," said the man in the red suit.

"That's incredible!" The man in the black suit was excited. "Sperm whales have a pair of 'lips' inside the end of their nose," he said. "No one knew what they were for. It looks like whales can use them to make sounds. Amazing!"

Other people came into the water with Physty. They touched him and petted him; they tried to get a sample of his blood so they could figure out what was wrong with him. Physty was sick and feeling terrible. He just wanted to be left alone.

Then a diver in a white suit came into the water with the others. He had a little plastic bucket and long cotton swabs. He took one of the swabs and gently touched the area around Physty's blowhole. Nothing had ever touched him there. Physty snorted.

"Easy, fella," said the diver in the white suit. "I want to take this to the lab. We can test it and find out what's the matter with you."

The red-suited diver reminded him: "Be gentle. This whale has never been touched by anything that wasn't his mother or his lunch."

The man in the black suit had been looking at Physty underwater. He said: "I can feel the pings; he's still trying to figure out what we are."

By this time, Physty had become a television star. All the stations had camera crews and reporters at Fire Island. Physty was the only live sperm whale the people of America had ever seen.

Interviewer: *"What can you tell us about Physty?"*

Scientist: *"Well, he's probably about five years old—"*

Interviewer: *"How do you know?"*

Scientist: *"He's about 25 feet long, and he has no teeth."*

Interviewer: *"No teeth? I thought sperm whales were supposed to have big ivory teeth; you know, the ones sailors made carvings out of."*

Scientist: *"Well, yes, but the teeth probably don't grow in until the whale is about ten years old."*

Interviewer: *"How old do sperm whales get?"*

Scientist: "We think they may get to be 60 or 70 years old."

Interviewer: "And how big do they get?"

Scientist: "Males get to be much larger than females, and the biggest males can be 60 feet long—about as long as five cars. A 60-foot whale weighs 60 tons—120,000 pounds."

Interviewer: "Are whales really intelligent?"

Scientist: "We don't know how intelligent. They are very good at being whales, but they probably aren't interested in doing people things, so we have no way of testing them."

Meanwhile, the scientists had examined the samples from Physty's blowhole at the lab. They discovered that the young whale had pneumonia. He had an infection in his lungs and it was making it hard for him to breathe.

Nobody knew how to help a whale with pneumonia. When people get pneumonia, doctors tell them to rest. They also give them medicine. Physty was already resting, so the veterinarians decided to give him a medicine that would knock out the infection. The vets wrapped a half-pound of medicine in a squid. Then they tried to force it into the corner of Physty's mouth.

Physty was not happy. All these red, white, and black creatures were swimming around him. They stuck things in his blowhole. Now they were trying to cram something into his mouth! Physty snorted, but he was too weak to do much else.

The divers got the food into Physty's mouth, and he swallowed it. He continued to rest in the shallow boat basin for almost a week. The television cameras recorded almost everything he did. The scientists watched him carefully. They noted how often he breathed, and they sketched his brown eyes. They were surprised to notice that Physty was more active at night than during the day. They wondered if sperm whales might stay awake at night and sleep during the day.

48

Things didn't look good for Physty. He was still having trouble breathing, and he hardly swam at all. He just lay on his right side with his left flipper tucked in and his blowhole out of the water. The scientists thought he was going to die. They knew that no large whale had *ever* survived being stranded. At the end of Physty's eighth day at the island, the scientists went to sleep. They thought that when they woke up the next morning, Physty would be dead.

But when they saw him the next day, Physty was swimming in circles around the boat basin! After a good night's sleep, he looked much better. His new friends decided to release him immediately.

A net had been strung across the entrance to the boat basin. Now that Physty was better, the man in the red diving suit cut the net. Everyone waited for Physty to swim to freedom. But he just stayed in the boat harbor, swimming in circles. The scientists and a veterinarian got into a rubber boat and herded Physty toward the ocean.

The crowd cheered as the little whale headed for his home, the open sea. When he was about five miles out, he threw his flukes into the air and dove beneath the waves.

Back on shore a little girl said, "Goodbye, Physty. I hope we never see you here again!"

TO LEARN MORE

If you'd like to learn more about sperm whales and other kinds of whales, you might try to find:

Whales, Dolphins and Porpoises of the World, by Mary L. Baker. Doubleday. New York. 1987.

The Book of Whales, by Richard Ellis. Alfred A. Knopf. New York. 1989.

Dolphins and Porpoises, by Richard Ellis. Alfred A. Knopf. New York. 1982.

The Sierra Club Handbook of Whales and Dolphins, by Stephen Leatherwood and Randall Reeves. Sierra Club Books. San Francisco. 1983.

The only whales in captivity are belugas. You can see them at the aquariums at Coney Island (New York), Chicago, Vancouver (Canada), and at various oceanariums, such as the Sea Worlds in San Diego (California) and Orlando (Florida). There are many places where you can see dolphins and killer whales, which are smaller cousins of the great whales.

Harbor porpoise

Killer whale

Bottlenose dolphin

White-sided dolphin

Pilot whale

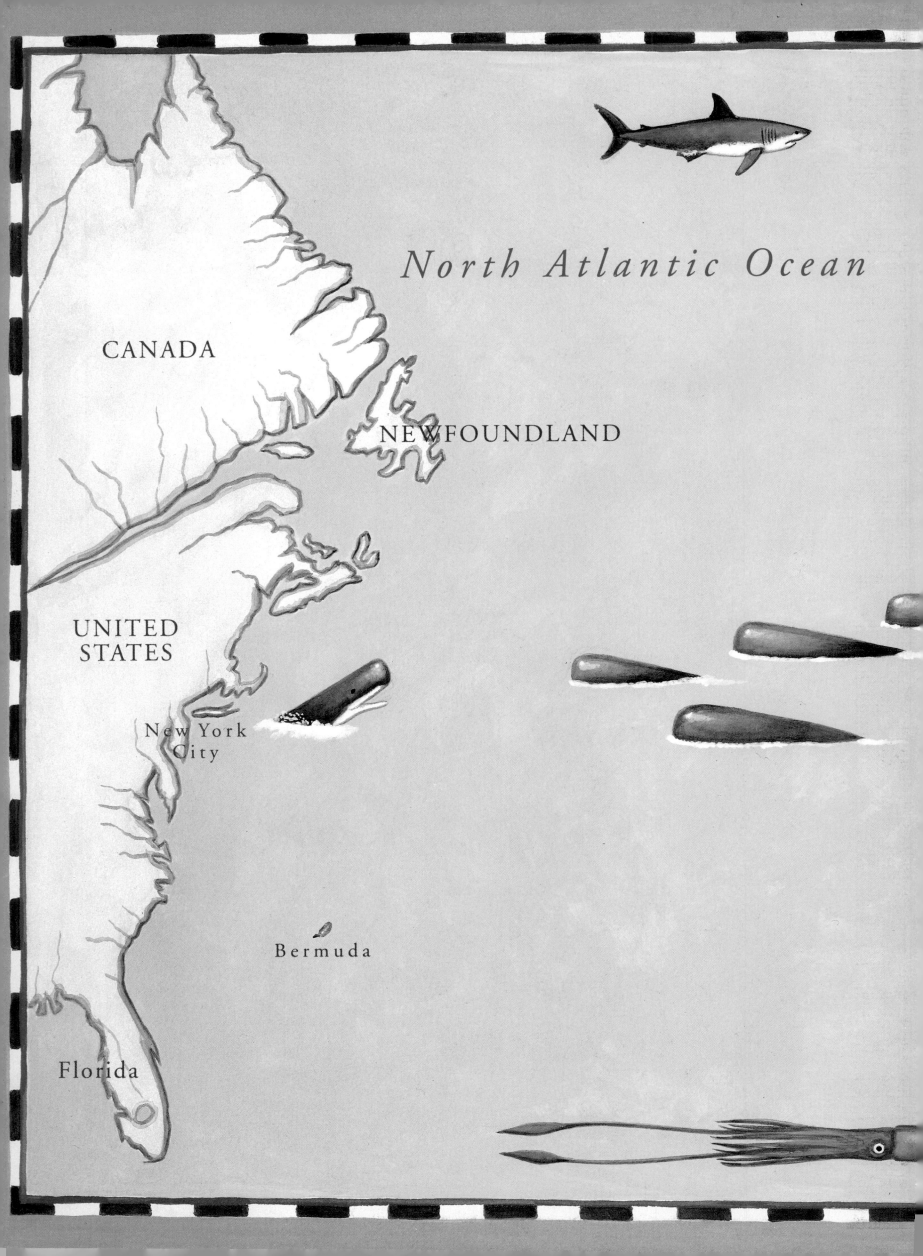

North Atlantic Ocean

CANADA

NEWFOUNDLAND

UNITED
STATES

New York
City

Bermuda

Florida